Political Cartoons Activities
for American History
with Answer Key

HOLT

American Anthem

HOLT, RINEHART AND WINSTON

A Harcourt Education Company

Orlando • **Austin** • New York • San Diego • London

Contents

Contents

The *Political Cartoons Activities for American History* provide content-related political cartoons to enrich and broaden instruction. Early political cartoon activities include instructional captions that guide students in interpreting symbolism, caricature, satire, and bias. Subsequent political cartoons contain captions only on those occasions when students would benefit from additional contextual clues. Critical thinking questions encourage further analysis and provide prompts for discussion. In addition, the *Teacher's Edition* provides references to help you integrate the political cartoon activities into the overall instruction.

Cartoon 1 | Political Cartoons

Here We Come

ANALYZING POLITICAL CARTOONS

Study the political cartoon, and then answer the questions that follow.

1. What is the significance of the flag in the cartoon?

____

____

2. Who do the people in the bushes at the right of the cartoon represent?

____

____

3. If the land in this cartoon is meant to represent the first place in the Americas where Columbus landed, what island is being portrayed?

____

____

Political Cartoons

The Spanish Arrive in the Americas

ANALYZING POLITICAL CARTOONS

Study the political cartoon, and then answer the questions that follow.

1. Who or what does the man represent?

____

____

2. What is the message of this political cartoon?

____

____

3. Do you think the cartoonist has a positive or negative view of the actions of the person or group that the man in the cartoon represents? Explain your answer.

____

____

Cartoon 3

Political Cartoons

Sir Walter Raleigh Returns from Another Voyage

In the cartoon, Sir Walter Raleigh is shown demonstrating bubble-gum for the British royal court. In reality, Sir Walter Raleigh brought back potatoes and tobacco from his explorations of the Americas and introduced their use in Europe.

www.CartoonStock.com

ANALYZING POLITICAL CARTOONS

Study the political cartoon, and then answer the questions that follow.

1. What accomplishments of Sir Walter Raleigh is the cartoon poking fun at?

____

____

2. Why would an explorer be eager to bring back something of value from his trips and share his discoveries with his monarch?

____

____

3. In 1587 Raleigh sent out an expedition that settled on Roanoke Island, off the coast of present-day North Carolina. What happened to this colony of settlers?

____

____

Cartoon 4   # Political Cartoons

No to Asylum Seekers

ANALYZING POLITICAL CARTOONS

Study the political cartoon, and then answer the questions that follow.

1. Who does the person holding the sign represent?

   ____

   ____

2. Who is aboard the ship that is shown?

   ____

   ____

3. The cartoonist portrays the person with the sign as having an anti-immigrant view. What point do you think the cartoonist is trying to make with this cartoon?

   ____

   ____

Colonists React to a Royal Appointment

The king appointed this Anglican bishop to lead the Congregationalists.

The Congregationalists are shouting, "No Lords Spiritual or Temporal in New England."

These people are Boston Congregationalists.

Library of Congress Prints and Photographs Division

ANALYZING POLITICAL CARTOONS

Study the political cartoon, and then answer the questions that follow.

1. Why might the Congregationalists be angry?

   ____

   ____

2. Why might the Congregationalists prefer a leader of the same religion?

   ____

   ____

3. What do you think is meant by the cry of "No Lords Spiritual or Temporal in New England"?

   ____

   ____

Cartoon 6 Political Cartoons

Rice Ready for Shipping

The barrels contain rice, which has been prepared for shipping.

© Bettmann/CORBIS

ANALYZING POLITICAL CARTOONS

Study the political cartoon, and then answer the questions that follow.

1. Who are the people working on the barrels?

   ____

   ____

2. How does the work of the men working on the barrels contrast with what the men on the left are doing?

   ____

   ____

3. Using what you have learned in your studies and the cartoon, to what location(s) do you think the rice is being shipped?

   ____

   ____

Cartoon 7

Political Cartoons

The Colonies Throw Britain

ANALYZING POLITICAL CARTOONS

Study the political cartoon, and then answer the questions that follow.

1. Why would the artist depict America as a bucking horse?

____

____

2. What is the significance of the American horse having a British rider?

____

____

3. Using what you have learned in your studies and the cartoon, what is represented by the whip the British rider is using?

____

____

Burial of the Stamp Act

ANALYZING POLITICAL CARTOONS

Study the political cartoon, and then answer the questions that follow.

1. What event is the cartoonist depicting by showing Parliament at a funeral and burial
   for the Stamp Act? What led to the "death" of the Stamp Act?

   ____

   ____

2. Why did Parliament feel sad when the Stamp Act was repealed?

   ____

   ____

WRITING ACTIVITY

Write a petition to Parliament protesting the Stamp Act. Be sure to include
the reasons why you believe this act should be repealed.

Cartoon 9   Political Cartoons

Announcing the Constitution

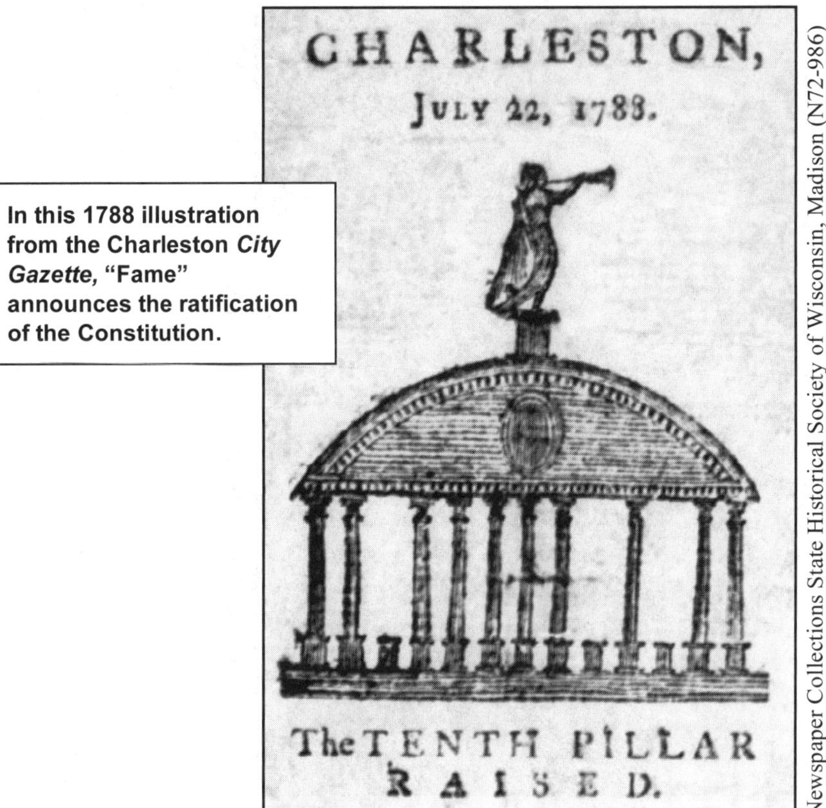

In this 1788 illustration from the Charleston *City Gazette,* "Fame" announces the ratification of the Constitution.

Newspaper Collections State Historical Society of Wisconsin, Madison (N72-986)

ANALYZING POLITICAL CARTOONS

Study the political cartoon, and then answer the questions that follow.

1. Who or what do the ten columns represent?

   ____

   ____

2. Three columns appear to be missing from this illustration. Who or what do they represent?

   ____

   ____

3. What is represented by the entire structure?

   ____

   ____

Political Cartoons

The Temple of Liberty

The cherub holds a
document titled
"Constitution."

ANALYZING POLITICAL CARTOONS

Study the political cartoon, and then answer the questions that follow.

1. Why would the artist depict a temple erected to honor "liberty, justice, and peace"?

   ____

   ____

2. What is the significance of the cherub holding the Constitution and pointing to the temple?

   ____

   ____

WRITING ACTIVITY

In three paragraphs, discuss how the Constitution was designed to help
ensure liberty, justice, and peace for U.S. citizens.

A Watchful Eye

The document in Jefferson's left hand is the U.S. Constitution.

On the vessel containing burning papers is inscribed "Altar to Gallic [French] Despotism."

Courtesy, American Antiquarian Society

ANALYZING POLITICAL CARTOONS

Study the political cartoon, and then answer the questions that follow.

1. The cartoon was meant to persuade potential voters in the presidential election of 1800 that Jefferson and his party—the Democratic Republicans—were dangerously pro-French, and that a Jefferson victory would bring the violence and chaos of the French Revolution to the United States. What conveys this message in the cartoon?

   ____

   ____

2. Some of Jefferson's political opponents accused him of wanting to destroy organized religion. What in the cartoon might be an indirect reference to this?

   ____

   ____

3. What do you think the eagle in the cartoon represents? Explain your answer.

   ____

   ____

Caught between Britain and France

From left to right, the figures shown are **King George of Britain, President Thomas Jefferson, and Emperor Napoleon of France.**

The Granger Collection, New York

ANALYZING POLITICAL CARTOONS

Study the political cartoon, and then answer the questions that follow.

1. This cartoon shows President Thomas Jefferson caught between King George and Napoleon during the time of the Napoleonic Wars, when France fought against Britain. Why do you think the cartoonist portrayed Jefferson in this way?

____

____

2. This cartoon appeared after President Thomas Jefferson proposed and Congress passed the Embargo Act in 1807. What do you think the cartoonist is trying to represent by showing money being ripped out of Jefferson's pants?

____

____

3. What incident involving British and American ships led to the Embargo Act?

____

____

Cartoon 13   Political Cartoons

Splitting Apart Enslaved Families

As the man on the table auctions off an infant slave, the slave's mother (shown kneeling) pleads with her owner to reconsider selling off her child.

©Fotomas / Topham/The Image Works

ANALYZING POLITICAL CARTOONS

Study the political cartoon, and then answer the questions that follow.

1. Based on the sign in the top left part of the cartoon, how is the cartoonist portraying the general attitude toward slavery in this part of America at the time of the cartoon?

____

____

2. Why might members of enslaved families be separated from each other?

____

____

3. Based on your readings about the South's economy, where will the African Americans shown here most likely be taken to work?

____

____

Cartoon 14   Political Cartoons

The Spoils System

ANALYZING POLITICAL CARTOONS

Study the political cartoon, and then answer the questions that follow.

1. Who is shown riding the hog?

   ____

   ____

2. Explain the statement, "To the Victors Belong the Spoils."

   ____

   ____

3. According to the cartoon, did the person depicted support or oppose the spoils
   system? Explain.

   ____

   ____

Cartoon 15   Political Cartoons

Attack on the Post Office, 1835

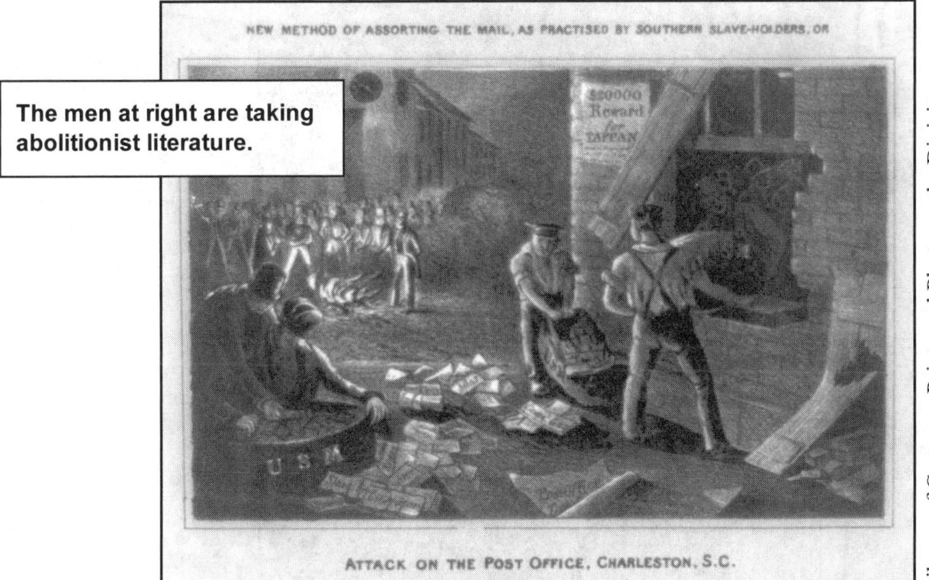

The men at right are taking abolitionist literature.

ANALYZING POLITICAL CARTOONS

Study the political cartoon, and then answer the questions that follow.

1. Who is shown raiding the mail at the post office in Charleston, South Carolina?

   ____

   ____

2. What are the people doing with the abolitionist literature?

   ____

   ____

WRITING ACTIVITY

In a paragraph, describe your reaction if you had been a witness to the events portrayed in this cartoon.

Cartoon 16   Political Cartoons

The Bar of Destruction

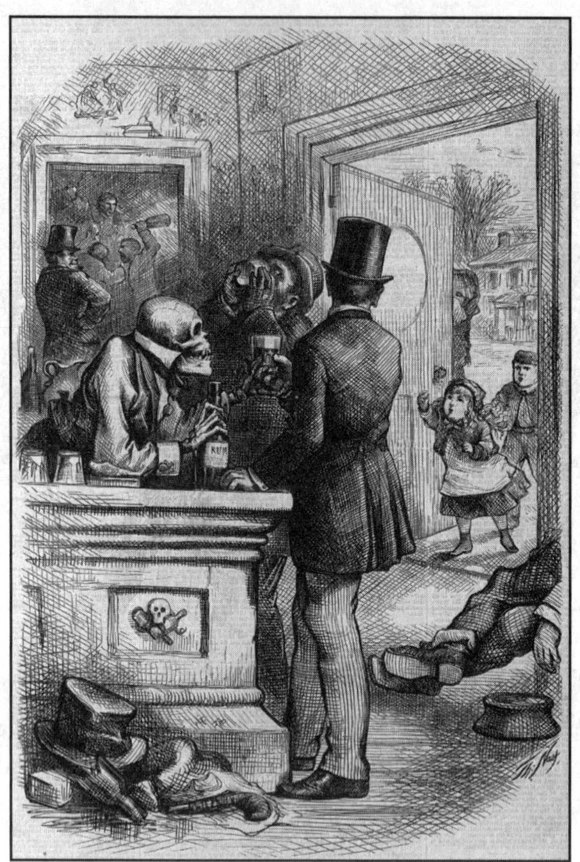

ANALYZING POLITICAL CARTOONS

Study the political cartoon, and then answer the questions that follow.

1. In this temperance cartoon, why do you think the cartoonist portrays the bartender as a skeleton?

   ____

   ____

2. What other aspects of the cartoon convey the negative effects of alcohol?

   ____

   ____

3. What do you think the cartoonist's intention was in showing the two children coming to the front door?

   ____

   ____

Annexation of Texas

This man urges Andrew Jackson to support James K. Polk and George Dallas—two pro-annexation Democrats—in their effort to become their party's candidates for president and vice president in the election of 1844.

Andrew Jackson is being led by Democrat Martin Van Buren, who was competing with James K. Polk for his party's nomination as its presidential candidate in the election of 1844. Since Van Buren opposed the extension of slavery he was against Texas annexation, but he tried to keep his position on the issue ambiguous.

ANALYZING POLITICAL CARTOONS

Study the political cartoon, and then answer the questions that follow.

1. What does the cartoon suggest about Andrew Jackson's influence in the Democratic Party at this time, years after he had left the presidency?

2. Why would Van Buren's opposition to slavery lead him to oppose Texas annexation?

3. Which of the candidates in the cartoon eventually won the Democratic nomination and then the presidency?

Political Cartoons

Volunteers for Texas

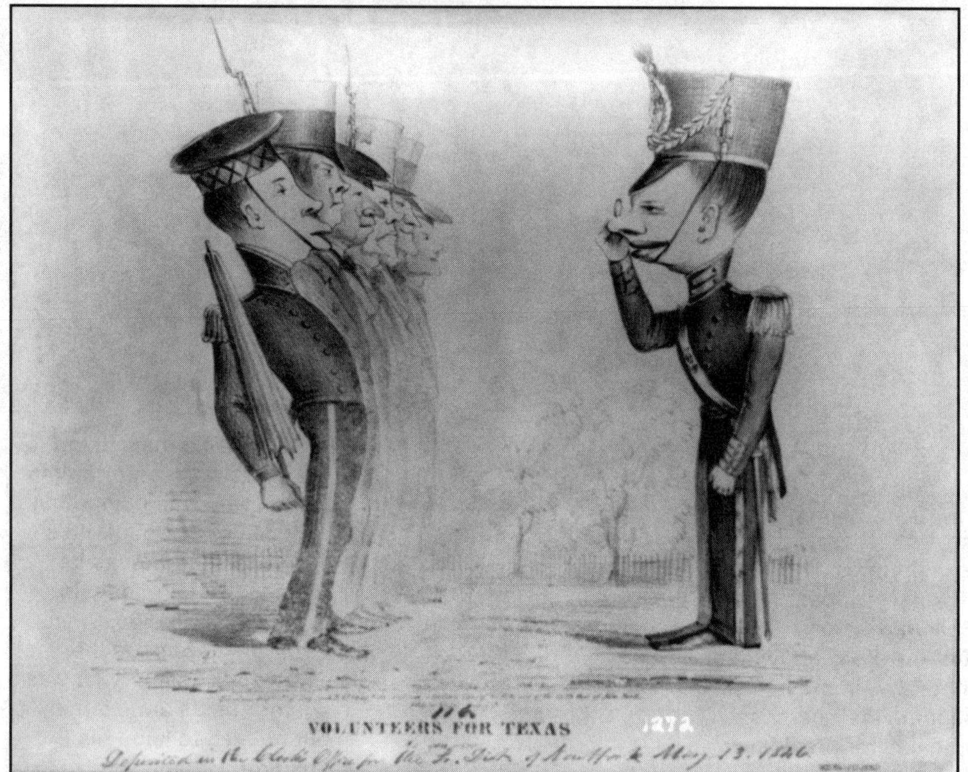

Library of Congress Prints and Photographs Division

ANALYZING POLITICAL CARTOONS

Study the political cartoon, and then answer the questions that follow.

1. Why is the first volunteer shown carrying an umbrella rather than a gun?

   ____

   ____

2. How does the artist portray the officer, and what does this portrayal suggest?

   ____

   ____

3. How does the title describe the cartoon?

   ____

   ____

Cartoon 19   Political Cartoons

Settlers Oppose Slavery

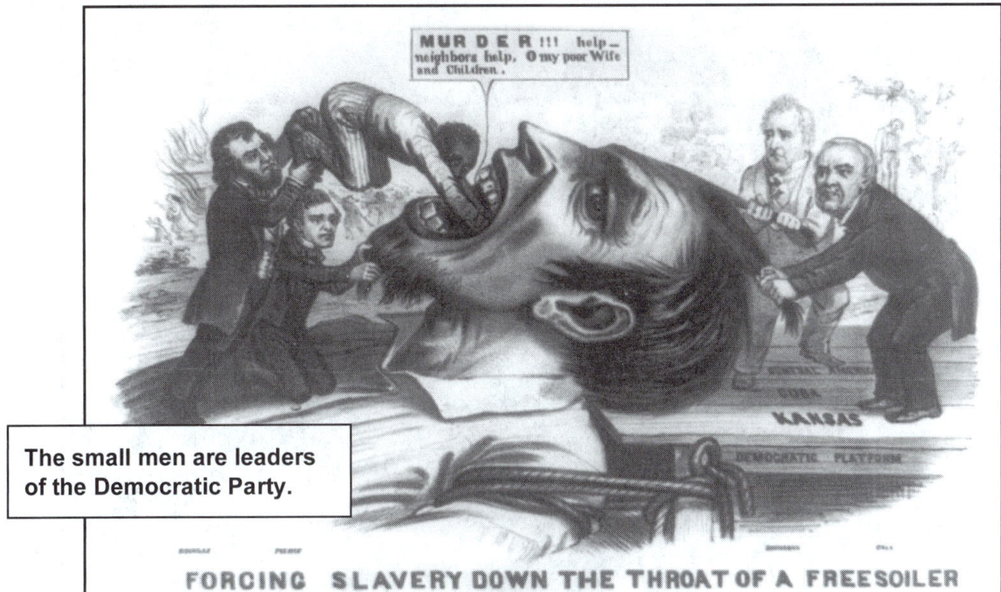

The small men are leaders of the Democratic Party.

Freesoilers opposed slavery in Kansas.

Library of Congress Prints and Photographs Division

ANALYZING POLITICAL CARTOONS

Study the political cartoon, and then answer the questions that follow.

1. Who or what does the man being held down represent?

____

____

2. Who or what is being forced into the man's mouth?

____

____

WRITING ACTIVITY

This cartoon accurately expresses how many opponents of slavery felt about the Kansas-Nebraska Act. Write a paragraph explaining why they might have felt this way.

The South Secedes

ANALYZING POLITICAL CARTOONS

Study the political cartoon, and then answer the questions that follow.

1. Notice the title. Who or what does the spider represent?

   ____

   ____

2. What is the significance of the size of the spider?

   ____

   ____

3. Does the artist seem to be for or against secession? Why?

   ____

   ____

Breaking the Rebellion

The other hammers are labeled "Skill," "Strategy," and the "Draft."

The man seated in the background holds a small hammer labeled "Compromise."

The man holding the animal marked "Rebellion" is Confederate President Jefferson Davis.

The men holding the sledgehammers and ax are President Lincoln and other Union leaders. Lincoln's ax is labeled "Emancipation Proclamation."

Library of Congress Prints and Photographs Division

ANALYZING POLITICAL CARTOONS

Study the political cartoon, and then answer the questions that follow.

1. Notice the caption, "Breaking That 'Backbone.'" How did the northern leaders intend to stop the rebellion?

   ____

   ____

2. What is the significance of the man seated in the background with the hammer marked "Compromise"?

   ____

   ____

WRITING ACTIVITY

In a paragraph, discuss one strategy used by the North to break the rebellion.

Southern "Volunteers"

ANALYZING POLITICAL CARTOONS

Study the political cartoon, and then answer the questions that follow.

1. Why did the Confederacy need more men to fight in the Civil War?

   ____

   ____

2. Notice the caption, "Southern 'Volunteers.'" Were the men shown volunteering?

   ____

   ____

3. Using what you have learned in your studies and this cartoon, what event do you believe this cartoon is responding to?

   ____

   ____

Cartoon 23   Political Cartoons

David and Goliath

<table>
<tr><td>The subject of this cartoon is the presidential election of 1872.</td><td></td><td>The heavily favored Ulysses S. Grant is depicted as Goliath.</td></tr>
</table>

This is Horace Greeley.

ANALYZING POLITICAL CARTOONS

Study the political cartoon, and then answer the questions that follow.

1. Which man in the cartoon is best equipped to fight?

____

____

2. What weapons or credentials gave Ulysses S. Grant the advantage in fighting the battle of a presidential election?

____

____

3. Who do you think the cartoonist supports for president? Why?

____

____

Carpetbaggers

ANALYZING POLITICAL CARTOONS

Study the political cartoon, and then answer the questions that follow.

1. Who were carpetbaggers?

____

____

2. Does the cartoon support or oppose the arrival of carpetbaggers? Explain your answer.

____

____

WRITING ACTIVITY

Write a paragraph explaining why someone might choose to become a carpetbagger.

Cartoon 25   # Political Cartoons

Indian Agent

Library of Congress Prints and Photographs Division

The package the Indian is
holding is labeled
"starvation rations." Each
bag hanging from the agent
is labeled "profits."

ANALYZING POLITICAL CARTOONS

Study the political cartoon, and then answer the questions that follow.

1. Why do you think the Indian looks sad and surprised?

____

____

2. How is the Indian agent gaining profits?

____

____

WRITING ACTIVITY

Native American children attending a new school built by the U.S.
government were required to speak English and wear Anglo-style dress.
Write a paragraph about what this experience might have been like from
the perspective of a Native American child.

African American Migration During and After Slavery

ANALYZING POLITICAL CARTOONS

Study the political cartoon, and then answer the questions that follow.

1. What is depicted in the circular inset at the top left of the cartoon?

____

____

____

2. Based on what you know about the Exodusters, where do think the people in the main portion of the cartoon are going?

____

____

3. How do the two events pictured in this cartoon differ?

____

____

The Atlantic Telegraph Cable

ANALYZING POLITICAL CARTOONS

Study the political cartoon, and then answer the questions that follow.

1. Who or what do the two men represent?

____

____

2. Why do you think the two men are shaking hands?

____

____

WRITING ACTIVITY

On August 16, 1858, Queen Victoria sent President Buchanan a congratulatory telegram through the line, to which he responded. Write your own message of congratulations and a response that focuses on what this accomplishment means.

The Railroad in California

ANALYZING POLITICAL CARTOONS

Study the political cartoon, and then answer the questions that follow.

1. Who or what does the octopus represent?

   ____

   ____

2. The cartoon portrays the octopus controlling the financial interests of other industries. What other industries are represented?

   ____

   ____

3. Who do you think is being portrayed in the eyes of the octopus?

   ____

   ____

Cartoon 29   Political Cartoons

Boss Tweed

The large box is a ballot box, where votes are cast.

ANALYZING POLITICAL CARTOONS

Study the political cartoon, and then answer the questions that follow.

1. What is meant by the caption, "That's What's the Matter"?

   ____

   ____

2. What is the artist suggesting in the cartoon?

   ____

   ____

WRITING ACTIVITY

Write a paragraph explaining why Boss Tweed wanted cartoons such as this one to be stopped.

Cartoon 30 Political Cartoons

Immigration

Library of Congress Prints and Photographs Division

ANALYZING POLITICAL CARTOONS

Study the political cartoon, and then answer the questions that follow.

1. Who or what does the tall man represent?

    ____

    ____

2. What does the artist think about immigration to the United States? How can you tell?

    ____

    ____

WRITING ACTIVITY

Using what you have learned in your studies and the cartoon, write two paragraphs detailing the reasons immigrants would leave their home countries to live in the United States during this time period, and the ways in which their lives would likely change as a result of their new citizenship.

The Wrestling Match

ANALYZING POLITICAL CARTOONS

Study the political cartoon, and then answer the questions that follow.

1. Who is shown wrestling with the railroad?

____

____

2. Why do you think the man is shown wrestling the railroad?

____

____

WRITING ACTIVITY

The Elkins and Hepburn Acts could be considered an outcome of the "wrestling match." How did they help regulate the railroad industry?

Make Way!

The Granger Collection, New York

ANALYZING POLITICAL CARTOONS

Study the political cartoon, and then answer the questions that follow

1. This 1912 cartoon about the women's suffrage movement was entitled "Make Way!"
   For whom or what do you think the cartoonist is saying to make way? Explain.

   ____

   ____

2. Why might this cartoon have been controversial when it was published, especially
   among men?

   ____

   ____

3. Which amendment, ratified in 1920, gave women nationwide the right to vote?

   ____

   ____

Cartoon 33   Political Cartoons

Pershing and Villa

Library of Congress Prints and Photographs Division

The man shown on the left is Pancho Villa. The man on the right is General John J. Pershing.

ANALYZING POLITICAL CARTOONS

Study the political cartoon, and then answer the questions that follow.

1. Why would the artist show General Pershing with an angry look on his face?

____

____

2. Why would the artist depict Pancho Villa with a smile on his face?

____

____

3. Why did the cartoonist use the term *punitive* to describe Pershing's expedition?

____

____

Political Cartoons

U.S. Imperialism

The Granger Collection, New York

ANALYZING POLITICAL CARTOONS

Study the political cartoon, and then answer the questions that follow.

1. Who or what does the eagle represent?

   ____

   ____

2. The cartoon was created in 1904 and shows U.S. flags planted in the Philippines, Panama, and Puerto Rico. What do the flags symbolize?

   ____

   ____

WRITING ACTIVITY

What were the three main reasons for U.S. imperialism?

Isolationism and World War I

ANALYZING POLITICAL CARTOONS

Study the political cartoon, and then answer the questions that follow.

1. What does the fence represent in this cartoon?

____

____

2. Considering that the cartoon was created in 1916, what is the cartoonist trying to convey? Be sure to look carefully for all of the clues given in the cartoon.

____

____

3. What is the figure in the window's reasoning behind not letting Rollo out of the yard? Who or what do the two figures represent?

____

____

The Gap in the Bridge

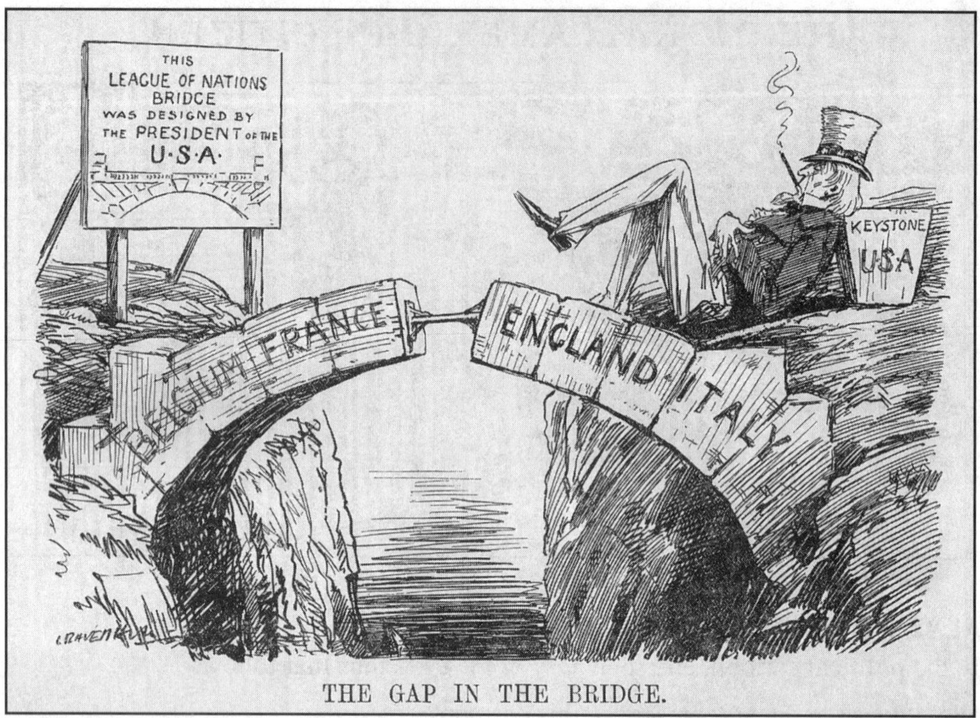

©Mary Evans Picture Library / The Image Works

ANALYZING POLITICAL CARTOONS

Study the political cartoon, and then answer the questions that follow.

1. What does the bridge in the cartoon represent?

____

____

2. What do the names of the countries on the bridge represent?

____

____

3. What is the cartoonist trying to convey by this cartoon?

____

____

Bolshevism

ANALYZING POLITICAL CARTOONS

Study the political cartoon, and then answer the questions that follow.

1. Who does the giant represent?

   ____

   ____

2. Does the cartoon support or oppose Bolshevism? Explain

   ____

   ____

3. Why are the clock hands shown attached to a globe?

   ____

   ____

Cartoon 38   Political Cartoons

Harding's Bid for Re-election

THE CANDIDATE FOR REELECTION.

"I'll have to figure out some kind of a new slogan."

—Alley in the Memphis *Commercial-Appeal.*

Courtesy of the Memphis Commercial Appeal

ANALYZING POLITICAL CARTOONS

Study the political cartoon, and then answer the questions that follow.

1. Why do you think the flag is tattered?

   ____

   ____

2. From looking at this cartoon, how would you describe Harding's state of mind?

   ____

   ____

3. Does this cartoon support or oppose Harding's re-election? Explain your answer.

   ____

   ____

The Eighteenth Amendment

©Mary Evans Picture Library / The Image Works

ANALYZING POLITICAL CARTOONS

Study the political cartoon, and then answer the questions that follow.

1. What items are showing up on the X-ray in this cartoon from 1923?

____

____

2. What is the cartoonist trying to convey about the Eighteenth Amendment?

____

____

WRITING ACTIVITY

Write a letter to the editor from the perspective of someone living during
the time of Prohibition, in which you make an argument for either keeping
Prohibition in place or repealing it.

Cartoon 40   Political Cartoons

The Nineteenth Amendment

ANALYZING POLITICAL CARTOONS

Study the political cartoon, and then answer the questions that follow.

1. On what is the woman standing? Why?

   ____

   ____

2. Why is the Nineteenth Amendment portrayed as a ladder in this cartoon?

   ____

   ____

3. What is meant by the caption of the cartoon, "The End of the Climb"?

   ____

   ____

Cartoon 41   Political Cartoons

Victim of Bank Failures

John T. McCutcheon, courtesy Tribune Media Services

ANALYZING POLITICAL CARTOONS

Study the political cartoon, and then answer the questions that follow.

1. Give some reasons why banks failed after the collapse of the stock market.

____

____

2. Who or what does the man represent?

____

3. What might the man have been thinking as he said, "I did"?

____

____

Hoover and the Depression

Picture History

ANALYZING POLITICAL CARTOONS

Study the political cartoon, and then answer the questions that follow.

1. What does President Hoover's exclamation, "Awful hard to quiet anything around here!" mean?

   ____

   ____

2. To which of the babies do the donkey's signs "Taint gonna rain no mo'!" and "Nobody knows how dry I am!" refer?

   ____

   ____

3. What was Hoover's philosophy about the role government should play in the Great Depression?

   ____

   ____

Cartoon 43 Political Cartoons

Farm Relief

ANALYZING POLITICAL CARTOONS

Study the political cartoon, and then answer the questions that follow.

1. Why was President Roosevelt's farm relief important?

____

____

2. Why do you think the farmer is expressing relief?

____

____

WRITING ACTIVITY

One of the steps taken to help farmers during the Depression was the creation of the Agricultural Adjustment Administration. This agency encouraged farmers to cut production in return for a subsidy. Use what you have learned in your readings to explain the logic behind this program.

A New Deal

© Scripps Howard News Service, image courtesy of FDR Library

ANALYZING POLITICAL CARTOONS

Study the political cartoon, and then answer the questions that follow.

1. Who or what is holding the cards? Explain your answer.

   ____

   ____

2. Why do you think the cartoon shows this person or entity holding the cards?

   ____

   ____

3. Notice the title. Why is the word "IS" capitalized? Explain your answer.

   ____

   ____

Lindbergh's View of World War II

ANALYZING POLITICAL CARTOONS

Study the political cartoon, and then answer the questions that follow.

1. What does the sea creature represent?

____

____

2. What elements of the cartoon reveal the cartoonist's doubts about Charles Lindbergh's position?

____

____

3. What do you think the landmass in the background represents? Explain.

____

____

                                    Political Cartoons

Uniting Americans for War

ANALYZING POLITICAL CARTOONS

Study the political cartoon, and then answer the questions that follow.

1. What actual event is this cartoon based on?

____

____

____

2. What does the "Disunited States" ship represent?

____

____

____

3. Why is Uncle Sam thanking the Japanese pilots?

____

____

Funding the War Effort

Mandeville Special Collections Library, University of California, San Diego

ANALYZING POLITICAL CARTOONS

Study the political cartoon, and then answer the questions that follow.

1. Who or what is represented by the animal in the cage?

____

____

2. Does the cartoon support or oppose the policies of the U.S. government? Explain.

____

____

3. Why might the U.S. government need the financial support of American citizens?

____

____

Cartoon 48   Political Cartoons

Allied Shipping

ANALYZING POLITICAL CARTOONS

Study the political cartoon, and then answer the questions that follow.

1. Which two leaders of the Allies are shown helping "Shipping"?

   ____

   ____

2. Explain what the cartoon represents.

   ____

   ____

3. By looking at the condition of the two fighters, do you think this cartoon was drawn early or late in the war? Explain.

   ____

   ____

Behind the Iron Curtain

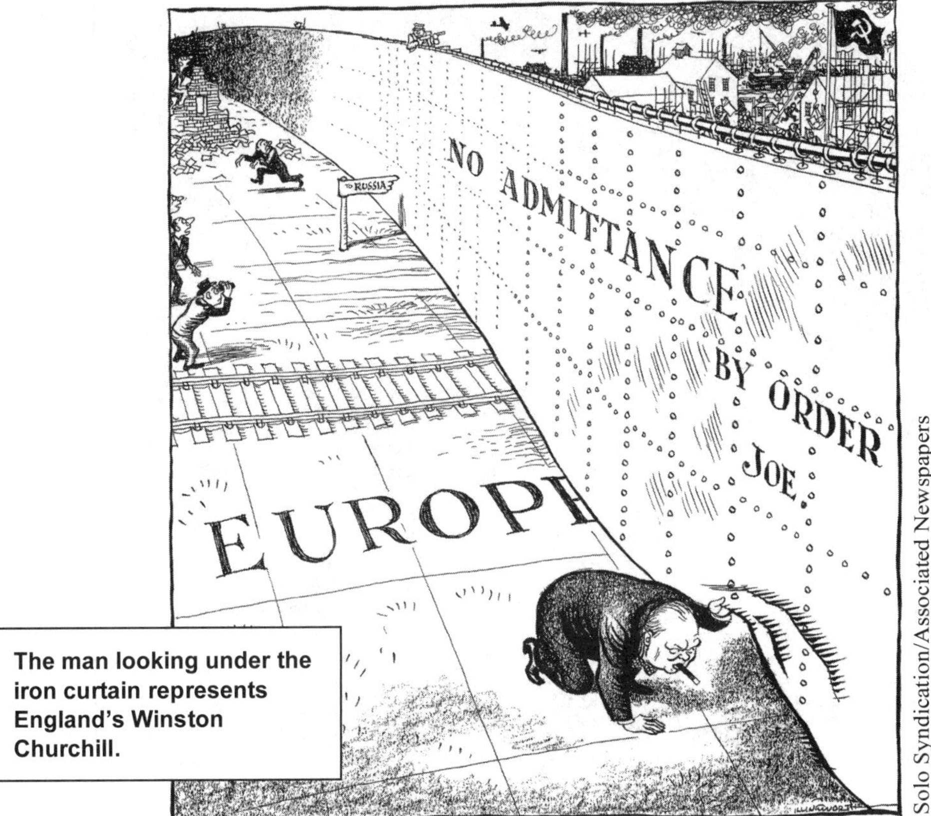

The man looking under the iron curtain represents England's Winston Churchill.

ANALYZING POLITICAL CARTOONS

Study the political cartoon, and then answer the questions that follow.

1. Notice the "No Admittance By Order Joe" sign on the Iron Curtain. Who is "Joe," and what country does he represent?

____

____

2. Why do you think Winston Churchill is shown peeping under the Iron Curtain?

____

____

3. Why do you think the artist shows the train tracks being cut off at the Iron Curtain?

____

____

Cartoon 50   # Political Cartoons

The Berlin Airlift

Giangreco, Airbridge to Berlin

ANALYZING POLITICAL CARTOONS

Study the political cartoon, and then answer the questions that follow.

1. What do the medals "coal" and "flour" represent?

   ____

   ____

2. Why do you think the artist shows the "coal" and "flour" medals as being as
   important as the other medals?

   ____

   ____

WRITING ACTIVITY

Write a few paragraphs describing what a West Berlin resident might have
felt when he or she saw the planes of the Berlin Airlift coming to deliver
supplies.

  Political Cartoons

I Like Ike

ANALYZING POLITICAL CARTOONS

Study the political cartoon, and then answer the questions that follow.

1. What are these buttons?

____

____

2. Why would the artist depict the buttons rolling downhill?

____

____

WRITING ACTIVITY

Create a political poster listing reasons why voters should support Eisenhower.

School Segregation

Copyright 1960 by Bill Mauldin. Displayed courtesy of the William Mauldin Estate

ANALYZING POLITICAL CARTOONS

Study the political cartoon, and then answer the questions that follow.

1. Why do you think the students are so small?

____

____

2. Does the artist's illustration seem to be saying that school segregation will continue or change? Why?

____

____

3. What is the artist saying with the title "Inch by Inch"?

____

____

Cartoon 53   # Political Cartoons

Kennedy and Khrushchev

Solo Syndication/Associated Newspapers

ANALYZING POLITICAL CARTOONS

Study the political cartoon, and then answer the questions that follow.

1. What event or events might have inspired the artist to create this cartoon?

   ____

   ____

2. Why is each man shown sitting on a missile from the other man's nation?

   ____

   ____

3. Other than the missiles, how does the artist portray the tension in this situation?

   ____

   ____

Cartoon 54   Political Cartoons

Johnson's Great Society

Reprinted from The Saturday Evening Post magazine, © 1969 Saturday Evening Post Society. Reprinted with permission.

ANALYZING POLITICAL CARTOONS

Study the political cartoon, and then answer the questions that follow.

1. Why do you think that the artist portrayed President Johnson with a bullhorn and musical instruments?

   ____

   ____

2. Who is pulling the plug?

   ____

   ____

3. Using your studies and this cartoon, when do you think it is most likely this cartoon was drawn and why?

   ____

   ____

Cartoon 55   Political Cartoons

Climbing Toward Equality

ANALYZING POLITICAL CARTOONS

Study the political cartoon, and then answer the questions that follow.

1. What do you think the thorn bush represents?

   ____

   ____

2. Notice the word "equality" on the rose. Why would the artist depict equality as a rose?

   ____

   ____

3. . Who is likely saying, 'Not so fast'?" in the quote at the bottom of the cartoon?

   ____

   ____

Cartoon 56   # Political Cartoons

The Montgomery Boycott

"Tote dat Barge! Lif dat boycott! Ride dat bus!" ---from *Herblock's Special for Today* (Simon & Schuster, 1958). Image courtesy of the Prints & Photographs Division, Library of Congress

ANALYZING POLITICAL CARTOONS

Study the political cartoon, and then answer the questions that follow.

1. Who or what does the man walking away represent?

____

____

2. Who or what does the man in the foreground represent?

____

____

3. Why do you think the man in the foreground is angry?

____

____

Cartoon 57   # Political Cartoons

Around in Circles

ANALYZING POLITICAL CARTOONS

Study the political cartoon, and then answer the questions that follow.

1. Notice the quotation, "Hope this is the right route!" Who is the speaker?

____

____

2. Why do you think the artist depicted the road to peace in Vietnam as having no clear direction?

____

____

3. Do you think the cartoon was drawn before or after the 1973 settlement between the United States, North Vietnam, and South Vietnam?

____

____

Political Cartoons

Fighting Two Wars at One Time

"There's money enough to support both of you…Now, Doesn't that make you feel better?" —-from Herblock: A Cartoonist's Life (Times Books, 1998)

ANALYZING POLITICAL CARTOONS

Study the political cartoon, and then answer the questions that follow.

1. Who is the man shown in this cartoon?

____

____

2. Explain what the cartoonist is trying to convey in this cartoon.

____

____

3. The woman at the left of the cartoon is identified as the "Vietnam War." If the cartoonist had decided to identify the woman at the right as another "war," he could have used the term for President Johnson's large anti-poverty campaign that he announced in January 1964. What was that term?

____

Cartoon 59

Political Cartoons

Bella Abzug

By Doug Marlette, Copyright, 1998, Tribune Media Services. Reprinted with permission]

ANALYZING POLITICAL CARTOONS

Study the political cartoon, and then answer the questions that follow.

1. What was Bella Abzug primarily known for?

____

____

2. In general, what point is the artist making in the cartoon?

____

____

3. What does the flattened gate suggest about Abzug?

____

____

César Chávez

ANALYZING POLITICAL CARTOONS

Study the political cartoon, and then answer the questions that follow.

1. Notice the changing expressions on the faces of the farmworkers. Why might the man standing beside César Chávez have a smile on his face?

____

____

2. How does the artist convey the difficult conditions under which field workers labored?

____

____

WRITING ACTIVITY

Create a flyer that persuades others to join the California grape boycott.

Cartoon 61

Political Cartoons

The Tape Tug-of-War

Reprinted from The Dallas Morning News. Copy courtesy of McCain Library and Archives, University of Southern Mississippi

ANALYZING POLITICAL CARTOONS

Study the political cartoon, and then answer the questions that follow.

1. Who is behind the closed door?

____

____

2. What information is on the tapes portrayed in the cartoon?

____

____

3. Why is the House Judiciary Committee pulling on the tapes?

____

____

Cartoon 62   Political Cartoons

Who Is Jimmy Kissinger?

Steve Greenberg, Daily News of Los Angeles, 1978

ANALYZING POLITICAL CARTOONS

Study the political cartoon, and then answer the questions that follow.

1. Why is President Carter pulling on the ties of Anwar Sadat and Menachem Begin?

____

____

2. Notice the caption, Jimmy Kissinger. Why would the artist refer to President Jimmy Carter as Jimmy Kissinger?

____

____

WRITING ACTIVITY

Develop a plan for bringing Menachem Begin and Anwar Sadat together for peace talks. Include how you would convince them to begin to talk. Use your studies and the cartoon to support your plan.

Cartoon 63   Political Cartoons

Strategic Defense Initiative

ANALYZING POLITICAL CARTOONS

Study the political cartoon, and then answer the questions that follow.

1. Who are the "Russkies" referred to in the cartoon?

   ____

   ____

2. Who is the captain of the Starship Ron?

   ____

   ____

3. Do you think the cartoon supports or opposes the Strategic Defense Initiative? Explain your answer.

   ____

   ____

Double Dip

© Paul Berge

ANALYZING POLITICAL CARTOONS

Study the political cartoon, and then answer the questions that follow.

1. To what events during President George H. W. Bush's presidency do the two "flavors" of ice cream that he is offering (Recession Crunch and Iraqi Road) refer?

   ____

   ____

2. Which of the "flavors" led to President Bush's political downfall?

   ____

   ____

WRITING ACTIVITY

Choose another important event that occurred during George Bush's presidency and write a paragraph that briefly describes the event and explains why it was significant.

A Close Shave

copyright 1998 by Herblock in The Washington Post

ANALYZING POLITICAL CARTOONS

Study the political cartoon, and then answer the questions that follow.

1. This cartoon was published in November 1998. What elected figure from that period was at risk of being led to the guillotine shown in the cartoon? Explain.

   ____

   ____

2. What do you think the cartoonist was trying to convey by having the figure identified as Congress asking, "What have we got that's more like a close shave?" Explain.

   ____

   ____

3. What was the result of the impeachment trial alluded to in the cartoon?

   ____

   ____

Political Cartoons

Bush and Social Security

ANALYZING POLITICAL CARTOONS

Study the political cartoon, and then answer the questions that follow.

1. Who is depicted in the cartoon?

   ____

   ____

2. Why do you think he is shown throwing a lighted match into papers that represent Social Security?

   ____

   ____

3. Why do you think his right hand is on the fire alarm?

   ____

   ____

Cartoon 1

Here We Come
ANALYZING POLITICAL CARTOONS

1. The flag signifies that Columbus is claiming the land for Spain.
2. Native Americans at the time of Columbus's arrival in the Americas
3. San Salvador

Cartoon 2

The Spanish Arrive in the Americas
ANALYZING POLITICAL CARTOONS

1. a Spanish conquistador
2. that the Spanish came to the Americas and destroyed much of the native culture of the Native Americans
3. Since the man is shown destroying Native American culture, and the background of the cartoon is so dark that it conveys a dark mood, the cartoonist does not have a positive view of the actions of the Spanish in the Americas.

Cartoon 3

Sir Walter Raleigh Returns from Another Voyage
ANALYZING POLITICAL CARTOONS

1. Sir Walter Raleigh brought back potatoes and tobacco from his explorations of the Americas and introduced their use in Europe.
2. Because most explorers were sponsored by a monarch who funded voyages in hopes of discovering new lands and riches, explorers would make showing their sponsor that they had found something of value a high priority.
3. No one knows. Roanoke's governor was called away to England for three years, and when he returned, the colony was in ruins and deserted, but no one has ever figured out what had happened to the colonists.

Cartoon 4

No to Asylum Seekers
ANALYZING POLITICAL CARTOONS

1. a Native American from 1620
2. the Pilgrims
3. Answers will vary. Possible answer: The cartoonist is trying to show that if the Native Americans in the 1620s had had the type of anti-immigrant views that some Americans have today, the Pilgrims—who were seeking asylum from religious persecution—would not have been able to settle in the Americas.

Cartoon 5

Colonists React to a Royal Appointment
ANALYZING POLITICAL CARTOONS

1. Answers will vary. The king has appointed a leader whose religious beliefs differ from those of the Congregationalists. People who value religious freedom probably would not want to be assigned a leader whose religion is different from their own.
2. Answers will vary. A leader who shares the followers' religion would probably lead in a manner that better satisfied the believers.
3. Answers will vary. Students may suggest they will accept no rule other than their own or that of God.

Cartoon 6

Rice Ready for Shipping
ANALYZING POLITICAL CARTOONS

1. They are probably enslaved people.
2. Answers will vary. The men on the left might be agreeing on terms of the sale or shipping of the rice, in contrast to the

difficult manual labor being performed by the African Americans.

3. Answers will vary. Students may suggest that the rice is being shipped to Great Britain or the northern colonies for trade.

Cartoon 7

The Colonies Throw Britain

ANALYZING POLITICAL CARTOONS

1. Like a horse attempting to throw off its rider, the colonies rebelled against arrogant British officials and openly disobeyed laws they did not like.

2. A person riding a horse tries to bring the horse under submission. The British, the rider in the picture, tried to bring the colonists into submission by passing a series of laws and acts.

3. The whip represents laws passed by British Parliament, including the Sugar, Stamp, Quartering, and Townshend Acts, and the Proclamation of 1763.

Cartoon 8

Burial of the Stamp Act

ANALYZING POLITICAL CARTOONS

1. The funeral symbolizes the repeal of the Stamp Act, which was so unpopular with colonists that it led to a boycott of British goods. After British merchants complained, Parliament responded by repealing the act, resulting in its demise.

2. Parliament initiated the Stamp Act to tax the colonies and raise money since the British government was severely in debt. This income source was lost when the Stamp Act was repealed. The members of Parliament might also be mourning their unlimited control over the colonists.

WRITING ACTIVITY

Students' petitions should include their reasons for wanting the Stamp Act to be repealed.

Cartoon 9

Announcing the Constitution

ANALYZING POLITICAL CARTOONS

1. the states that had, up to that time, ratified the Constitution

2. the states that had not ratified the Constitution

3. the federal government or the Constitution

Cartoon 10

The Temple of Liberty

ANALYZING POLITICAL CARTOONS

1. This celebrates the hope that these benefits will come to the nation because of the Constitution.

2. This indicates the belief that the Constitution is the way to achieve liberty, justice, and peace.

WRITING ACTIVITY

Students' paragraphs should discuss how the Constitution will help ensure liberty, justice, and peace for its citizens.

Cartoon 11

A Watchful Eye

ANALYZING POLITICAL CARTOONS

1. Jefferson is shown as sacrificing the U.S. Constitution on the "Altar of Gallic Despotism."

2. the eye of God—in the top right of the cartoon—keeping a close watch on Jefferson

3. Answers will vary. Possible answer: The eagle probably represents the United States, in the form of the American people, who have to be vigilant concerning Jefferson and who can prevent his sacrificing the Constitution by not voting for him for president.

Cartoon 12

Caught between Britain and France

ANALYZING POLITICAL CARTOONS

1. because the United States, in a sense, was caught between the British and the French during the Napoleonic Wars, which adversely affected U.S. trade with the two countries
2. Because of the Embargo Act, American merchants lost a lot of money since they were not allowed to export goods to any foreign country.
3. the *Chesapeake* incident

Cartoon 13

Splitting Apart Enslaved Families

ANALYZING POLITICAL CARTOONS

1. that it was an everyday part of life in which slaves were considered to be property and were bought and sold the same way as horses and cattle
2. Answers will vary, but students might say that if splitting up an enslaved family was the best way to make a profit, most slave owners would not hesitate to do so.
3. They will most likely be working in cotton fields.

Cartoon 14

The Spoils System

ANALYZING POLITICAL CARTOONS

1. Andrew Jackson
2. *Victors* refers to Jackson's political supporters. *Spoils* refers to public offices that were awarded to political supporters.
3. Answers will vary, but students might say that Jackson's proud demeanor while astride the hog, along with the quote on the statue's plaque that is attributed to

him, strongly suggest that he supported the spoils system.

Cartoon 15

Attack on the Post Office, 1835

ANALYZING POLITICAL CARTOONS

1. people such as slaveholders who did not agree with abolitionism
2. They are burning it.

WRITING ACTIVITY

Students' paragraphs should describe their reactions if they had witnessed the events portrayed in the cartoon.

Cartoon 16

The Bar of Destruction

ANALYZING POLITICAL CARTOONS

1. to show the deadly danger of alcohol
2. The men in the back room are in the middle of a fight in which one man is about to strike another with a bottle; one man at the bar is downing a drink in a desperate way, as if to suggest that he has an alcohol problem; the man in the lower right corner is slouched on a chair in rumpled clothing, asleep or at least unproductive as a result of drinking alcohol.
3. Answers will vary. Possible answer: They are shown coming to get their father, who has probably spent too much time—and possibly money—at the bar and is needed at home. The cartoonist's intent was probably to show that drinking alcohol affects not only the men who are shown in the cartoon, but their families as well.

Cartoon 17

Annexation of Texas

ANALYZING POLITICAL CARTOONS

1. The cartoon suggests that it is still strong, since people are competing for Jackson's

support of their candidates in the contest for the Democratic Party's nomination.
2. because the annexation of Texas would spread slavery westward and increase slave slates' voting power in Congress
3. James K. Polk

Cartoon 18
Volunteers for Texas
ANALYZING POLITICAL CARTOONS
1. This emphasizes how unprepared for battle the volunteers were.
2. The officer is young, and inspects the volunteers through a monocle. This suggests inexperience.
3. Answers will vary. The volunteers were unprepared to fight because they had no uniforms or weapons like a well-organized army would have. However, they were ready to volunteer. They wanted to fight for Texas.

Cartoon 19
Settlers Oppose Slavery
ANALYZING POLITICAL CARTOONS
1. Kansas settlers who oppose slavery
2. slavery

WRITING ACTIVITY
Students' paragraphs should explain why opponents of slavery felt the way they did about the Kansas-Nebraska Act.

Cartoon 20
The South Secedes
ANALYZING POLITICAL CARTOONS
1. the attempted secession of the southern states
2. The large size of the spider represents the significant threat posed by secession.
3. Answers will vary. Students may say the cartoonist is against secession as the cartoon shows the spider threatening the

peace and plenty of the country. The dropped sickle may indicate the impact the secession would have on the North as farming was a major occupation of the South.

Cartoon 21
Breaking the Rebellion
ANALYZING POLITICAL CARTOONS
1. by using strategies identified on the sledgehammers—Skills, Strategy, Draft, and the Emancipation Proclamation
2. Compromise was no longer considered an option.

WRITING ACTIVITY
Students' paragraphs should discuss one of the North's strategies for breaking the rebellion.

Cartoon 22
Southern "Volunteers"
ANALYZING POLITICAL CARTOONS
1. They needed as many men as possible to take on the North, which had a larger population.
2. No, the Confederacy was forcing men to serve in the army.
3. the enactment by the Confederate Congress of a military draft, or conscription, in April 1862

Cartoon 23
David and Goliath
ANALYZING POLITICAL CARTOONS
1. Goliath, who represents Grant
2. Grant was a military hero, had served one term as president, and was popular with the voters.
3. Answers will vary. Students may respond that, although not the popular favored candidate, the cartoonist supports Greeley, because in the Bible David slew Goliath.

Cartoon 24

Carpetbaggers

ANALYZING POLITICAL CARTOONS

1. Northern Republicans who came to take part in the political and economic recovery of the South
2. It opposes their arrival, as shown by the symbol of the South being crushed by the carpetbag.

WRITING ACTIVITY

Students' paragraphs should mention what carpetbaggers hoped to accomplish by moving South. Possible answers may include profit motives or a desire to help others rebuild.

Cartoon 25

Indian Agent

ANALYZING POLITICAL CARTOONS

1. The person who is supposed to protect the Indian's interest is not doing a good job; he has provided very little help, as depicted in the small "Sioux nation rations" package the Indian holds, while at the same time walking away with wealth made from the Indians.
2. He is gaining profits by cheating the Indian. This was often achieved by selling productive land and giving the less productive land to the Indians.

WRITING ACTIVITY

Students' paragraphs will vary, but may mention the unfamiliar language, clothing, and rules experienced by a Native American child first attending a new U.S. government school.

Cartoon 26

African American Migration During and After Slavery

ANALYZING POLITICAL CARTOONS

1. an enslaved person escaping through a swamp to the North and freedom
2. They were probably heading west to settle in Kansas, Missouri, Indiana, or Illinois.
3. The slave in the circular inset crouches in fear as he hides from the boat in his attempt to avoid capture on his way to freedom; the African Americans in the main cartoon travel openly via boat.

Cartoon 27

The Atlantic Telegraph Cable

ANALYZING POLITICAL CARTOONS

1. the United States and Great Britain
2. To show a spirit of cooperation and goodwill between the two nations.

WRITING ACTIVITY

Students should write a message and reply that focuses on the completion of the telegraph cable between Great Britain and the United States and what it means for these two countries.

Cartoon 28

The Railroad in California

ANALYZING POLITICAL CARTOONS

1. the railroad monopoly
2. Answers may include farmers, lumber companies, shipping companies, miners, fruit growers, stage line companies, and the wine industry
3. Answers may vary, but students should suggest they are the monopolists of the time connected to the railroad, such as Cornelius Vanderbilt and Andrew Carnegie.

Cartoon 29

Boss Tweed

ANALYZING POLITICAL CARTOONS

1. This pro-voting slogan (In Counting There Is Strength) is rendered meaningless by Boss Tweed's control of elections.

2. Tweed, head of Tammany Hall, used his position to control elections.

WRITING ACTIVITY

Students' paragraphs should explain how cartoons such as these contributed to a negative public opinion of Boss Tweed.

Cartoon 30

Immigration

ANALYZING POLITICAL CARTOONS

1. Uncle Sam—i.e., the United States
2. The cartoonist is concerned about the large number of immigrants entering the United States. The immigrants are pictured as members of undesirable groups (the poor, political dissidents, and criminals) who wear angry, desperate expressions.

WRITING ACTIVITY

Students' paragraphs will vary, but should include increased economic opportunities letters should include their reasons for coming to the United States, how they think life will change, and their dreams for the future.

Cartoon 31

The Wrestling Match

ANALYZING POLITICAL CARTOONS

1. President Theodore Roosevelt
2. President Roosevelt focused his attention on regulating large corporations and on protecting consumers. Railroads were large corporations, dominating railroad shipping by eliminating competition and by granting rebates to other large corporations.

WRITING ACTIVITY

The Elkins Act prohibited railroads from accepting rebates, ensuring that all customers paid the same rates for shipping their products. The Hepburn Act strengthened the Interstate Commerce Commission (ICC), giving it the power to set maximum railroad rates.

Cartoon 32

Make Way!

ANALYZING POLITICAL CARTOONS

1. The cartoonist is saying to make way for women voters and women candidates. All of the people carrying signs are women, and their signs and sashes all either argue for a woman's right to vote or advocates voting for women.
2. Answers will vary. Women's suffrage was a controversial issue at the time, and there was significant opposition to the idea. In addition, by showing only men being pushed off the Earth, the cartoon may have been considered sexist or unfair. It may have especially offended men who were supporters of women's suffrage. Also, in advocating voting for only women, the cartoon could be interpreted as suggesting that candidates should be elected solely on the basis of their gender rather than on their qualifications.
3. the Nineteenth Amendment

Cartoon 33

Pershing and Villa

ANALYZING POLITICAL CARTOONS

1. Pershing was probably angry because he was unable to capture Pancho Villa.
2. He was laughing in Pershing's face, taunting him because the U.S. military could not capture him.
3. President Wilson ordered Pershing on a military expedition to Mexico to capture Pancho Villa so that the U.S. government could punish him for the killing of U.S. citizens in Columbus, New Mexico.

Cartoon 34

U.S. Imperialism

ANALYZING POLITICAL CARTOONS

1. The eagle represents the United States.
2. The flags symbolize areas of U.S. power

and influence. After its victory in the Spanish-American War, the United States took control of Puerto Rico and the Philippines as territories. In 1903 the United States supported the revolution in Colombia that resulted in Panamanian independence.

WRITING ACTIVITY

The three main reasons were economic (desire for new markets and raw materials), military (desire for naval bases and coaling stations), and ideological (sense of nationalism, and a desire to bring western-style culture, democracy, and Christianity to other cultures).

Cartoon 35

Isolationism and World War I
ANALYZING POLITICAL CARTOONS

1. the boundaries of the United States
2. that the United States, and specifically the U.S. Senate—in the form of the "Senatorial Granny"—were in an isolationist mood and were not willing to enter World War I
3. The figure is afraid that Rollo will get hurt if he ventures out of the yard. The figure in the window represents the Senate, and Rollo represents either America or the young men of America who would be called on to fight if the United States entered World War I.

Cartoon 36

The Gap in the Bridge
ANALYZING POLITICAL CARTOONS

1. the League of Nations
2. countries that have already joined the League of Nations
3. that for the League of Nations to be complete, the United States must become a member

Cartoon 37

Bolshevism
ANALYZING POLITICAL CARTOONS

1. Bolshevism
2. The cartoon opposes Bolshevism by showing that it would be a setback to liberty and progress.
3. This represents the threat that Bolshevism poses to liberty and progress throughout the world.

Cartoon 38

Harding's Bid for Reelection
ANALYZING POLITICAL CARTOONS

1. During his first election campaign, Harding promised a return to "normalcy," but his first term was marred by the Teapot Dome scandal and other bribery schemes by friends he appointed to lower level government posts.
2. Harding seems confused, and perhaps a bit frustrated.
3. It opposes Harding's re-election by mocking Harding's promise to bring back normalcy to America.

Cartoon 39

The Eighteenth Amendment
ANALYZING POLITICAL CARTOONS

1. bottles of alcohol
2. that many people flouted the law by continuing to drink alcohol, although secretly

WRITING ACTIVITY

Students should write a letter to the editor from the perspective of someone living in the time of Prohibition in which they argue for either maintaining Prohibition or repealing it.

Cartoon 40

The Nineteenth Amendment
ANALYZING POLITICAL CARTOONS

1. She is standing on top of a ballot box to represent that through the passage of the Nineteenth Amendment, women nationwide had won the right to vote.
2. In the cartoon, the woman used the ladder to get to the top of the ballot box, which symbolizes that passage of the Nineteenth Amendment is what enabled women to cast their ballots in elections.
3. "Climb" is used as a metaphor for the long struggle that women had to endure before they reached their goal of winning the right to vote.

Cartoon 41

Victim of Bank Failures
ANALYZING POLITICAL CARTOONS

1. Depositors withdrew their money; there was no deposit insurance and little cash on hand; many banks had themselves invested in the stock market; investors failed to repay loans.
2. People who believed that their bank accounts would be safe.
3. Answers will vary. Possible answers include "How could this have happened?" "How could I have lost everything?" "I did everything right, and I still lost all my money."

Cartoon 42

Hoover and the Depression
ANALYZING POLITICAL CARTOONS

1. It means that at the same time that the business depression, drought damage, and tariff are in need of attention, Democrats are loudly mocking Hoover's inability to deal with these issues.
2. drought damage

3. He believed that government should play as little role as possible, that government should not provide direct aid but should find ways to help the people help themselves.

Cartoon 43

Farm Relief
ANALYZING POLITICAL CARTOONS

1. Agriculture made up a substantial portion of the economy. It was vital to the economic recovery of the United States.
2. Unlike the previous administration, Roosevelt wanted to provide direct relief to ordinary citizens, to those at the bottom of the economic pyramid, which included farmers.

WRITING ACTIVITY

Because of reduced demand for farm products during the Depression, there was an oversupply of these products, which led to very low prices for them. If the government paid farmers a subsidy to reduce their production, then the resulting decreased supply would theoretically come into better balance with the reduced demand. This would eventually cause prices for farm products— and thus farmers' earnings—to rise.

Cartoon 44

A New Deal
ANALYZING POLITICAL CARTOONS

1. The U.S. government is holding the cards, as evidenced by the "US" on the cuff links and the stars on the sleeve.
2. This portrays the government as having the power to pass laws to regulate the banking industry.
3. Regulating the banking industry was a drastic change from the banking policies of the Hoover administration, and the capitalization of "IS" reflects the scope and importance of this change.

Cartoon 45

Lindbergh's View of World War II

ANALYZING POLITICAL CARTOONS

1. Nazi Germany
2. The sea creature is frighteningly enormous and is swimming from the direction of the smoking landmass that represents Europe.
3. It represents a smoldering Europe at war. This can be deduced from the fact that in 1941, Europe was already engulfed in war, and since the sea creature represents Nazi Germany, and its tail is resting on the piece of land across the water from the United States, that land represents Europe.

Cartoon 46

Uniting Americans for War
ANALYZING POLITICAL CARTOONS

1. the Japanese attack on Pearl Harbor
2. The ship represents the different reasons why some people in the United States did not support U.S. entry into World War II, causing disunity between those who thought that the United States should enter the war and those who believed that the United States should stay out of it.
3. The Japanese attack on Pearl Harbor galvanized American support for war against Japan and united nearly all Americans in the World War II effort.

Cartoon 47

Funding the War Effort
ANALYZING POLITICAL CARTOONS

1. Hitler or Nazi Germany
2. It supports the government's bond program by urging people to buy savings bonds and stamps.
3. The cost of fighting a huge war in both Europe and the Pacific was incredibly expensive and threatened to overwhelm the federal budget.

Cartoon 48

Allied Shipping
ANALYZING POLITICAL CARTOONS

1. President Franklin Roosevelt and British Prime Minister Winston Churchill
2. The cartoon represents the trouble that Allied shipping was having in the early part of the war because of the successful attacks that German U-boats were launching against Allied supply ships. President Roosevelt and British Prime Minister Churchill are shown trying to revive Allied shipping, which they did once American shipyards began producing ships at an amazing rate and the Allies began using these additional ships in convoys that helped protect against U-boat attacks.
3. It was probably drawn early in the war because "U-boats" seems to be winning. As the war progressed, Allied shipping became less vulnerable to U-boat attacks.

Cartoon 49

Behind the Iron Curtain
ANALYZING POLITICAL CARTOONS

1. Joseph Stalin from the Soviet Union
2. Churchill did not trust Stalin because Stalin was increasing the Soviet Union's influence in Europe.
3. Answers will vary, but students should discuss that separation of the Iron Curtain countries from the rest of Europe included economics and commerce.

Cartoon 50

The Berlin Airlift
ANALYZING POLITICAL CARTOONS

1. These are medals received for delivering supplies to the people of West Berlin during the Berlin Airlift.
2. Answers will vary, but students might say that the flights of the Berlin Airlift were in

many ways as dangerous, risky, and important as combat missions. They might also mention the humanitarian effort of the mission was being honored.

WRITING ACTIVITY

Student answers will vary, but should include descriptions of what a resident of West Berlin might have felt (e.g., gratitude, relief, happiness) upon receiving supplies and perhaps his or her reaction to the soldiers and countries delivering them.

Cartoon 51

I Like Ike
ANALYZING POLITICAL CARTOONS

1. They are political buttons supporting Dwight D. Eisenhower's run for the presidency.
2. The buttons rolling downhill represent Eisenhower's popularity gaining momentum and overtaking his competitors.

WRITING ACTIVITY

Students should create a political poster listing reasons why voters should support Eisenhower.

Cartoon 52

School Segregation
ANALYZING POLITICAL CARTOONS

1. Answers will vary. Students might say that the size of the students indicate their vulnerability in this issue.
2. The artist is showing that segregation will eventually end, as illustrated by the fact that the segregation door is now open slightly.
3. It will take time and effort to make progress toward integrating schools; it will likely happen in small increments rather than overnight.

Cartoon 53

Kennedy and Khrushchev
ANALYZING POLITICAL CARTOONS

1. The inspiration is likely the Cuban missile crisis and the arms race between the United States and the Soviet Union.
2. This shows that each nation is capable of destroying the other with nuclear weapons.
3. Tension is depicted by the droplets of sweat, the action of the arm wrestling, and the hovering of the leaders' fingers over the detonation buttons.

Cartoon 54

Johnson's Great Society
ANALYZING POLITICAL CARTOONS

1. The Great Society was Johnson's plan for the nation, and he wanted to "drum up" support for it.
2. Uncle Sam, who represents opposition to Johnson's Great Society.
3. Answers will vary, but students should suggest that this cartoon was drawn in 1966 or later. It was during the midterm elections that the Republicans gained seats. This cartoon could have been created before the elections, in order to sway people that it was time to stop Johnson. It was more likely created after this to indicate that people were no longer listening to Johnson.

Cartoon 55

Climbing Toward Equality
ANALYZING POLITICAL CARTOONS

1. Answers will vary. Students might say that it represents the difficult and dangerous path African Americans have had to take on the way to equality.
2. The rose, or equality, is beautiful and fragile. It is worth enduring danger and hardship to achieve it.

3. Americans who resisted equal rights for African Americans.

Cartoon 56

The Montgomery Boycott
ANALYZING POLITICAL CARTOONS

1. The man represents African Americans boycotting, or refusing to ride, the buses in Montgomery, Alabama.
2. The white citizenry of Montgomery who resisted equal rights for African Americans.
3. The boycott hurt the bus system financially. He is also upset because African Americans are refusing to accept what he sees as their proper role in society.

Cartoon 57

Around in Circles
ANALYZING POLITICAL CARTOONS

1. the United States
2. There were many attempts to reach peace, but most failed. No one seemed to agree on a strategy for achieving peace.
3. It was drawn before, because a settlement was eventually reached.

Cartoon 58

Fighting Two Wars at One Time
ANALYZING POLITICAL CARTOONS

1. President Lyndon B. Johnson
2. The cartoonist is trying to show that President Johnson is spending so much time and money on the Vietnam War that he is neglecting U.S. urban needs, despite Johnson's claim that he has enough money to spend on both problems.

Cartoon 59

Bella Abzug
ANALYZING POLITICAL CARTOONS

1. Bella Abzug was a U.S. Representative known for her efforts in the equal rights movement.
2. That fighting for equal rights was a positive thing, and rewarded with admission into heaven.
3. That she was a forceful advocate, not allowing anyone or anything to stand in the way of what she wanted.

Cartoon 60

César Chávez
ANALYZING POLITICAL CARTOONS

1. He has an expression of hope, thanks to Chávez's work to improve the lives and working conditions of farmworkers.
2. The hard physical effort is captured in the way the workers are bent over, concentrating on their work.

WRITING ACTIVITY
Students' flyers should include reasons for joining the grape boycott.

Cartoon 61

The Tape Tug-of-War
ANALYZING POLITICAL CARTOONS

1. Richard Nixon
2. The tapes contain all conversations held in Nixon's offices—including conversations regarding the Watergate scandal.
3. The committee believed that the tapes contained information on Nixon's role in the Watergate break-in and cover-up. They are pulling on the tapes because Nixon did not want to give them up.

Cartoon 62

Who Is Jimmy Kissinger?
ANALYZING POLITICAL CARTOONS

1. He wanted to encourage them to discuss peace proposals.
2. Answers will vary, but students might say that this is a reference to Henry Kissinger's earlier diplomatic successes.

WRITING ACTIVITY

Students' plans for bringing Menachem Begin and Anwar Sadat together for peace talks should include how they convince them to begin to talk.

Cartoon 63

Strategic Defense Initiative
ANALYZING POLITICAL CARTOONS

1. Russians; the Soviet Union
2. President Ronald Reagan
3. It opposes it, as illustrated in the caption "Another 'Giant Leap for Mankind'—Backwards."

Cartoon 64

Double Dip
ANALYZING POLITICAL CARTOONS

1. Recession Crunch refers to the U.S. recession that began in late 1990, and Iraqi Road refers to the Persian Gulf War, in which a U.S.-led coalition fought Iraqi forces to liberate Kuwait.
2. Recession Crunch

WRITING ACTIVITY

Students' paragraphs should briefly describe an important event that occurred during George Bush's presidency and explain why it was significant.

Cartoon 65

A Close Shave
ANALYZING POLITICAL CARTOONS

1. President Bill Clinton was facing the prospect of impeachment, represented by the guillotine in this cartoon.
2. Answers will vary. The cartoonist might have been trying to convey that approving articles of impeachment is a very serious matter and that the alleged offenses of President Clinton may not have warranted such a measure. However, the cartoon seems to have been suggesting that Congress should reprimand President Clinton in some other way.
3. President Clinton was acquitted when less than two-thirds of the Senate voted to convict him at his impeachment trial.

Cartoon 66

Bush and Social Security
ANALYZING POLITICAL CARTOONS

1. President George W. Bush
2. Answers will vary. Students might say that the artist believes that Bush's proposed changes in the Social Security program would be disastrous.
3. Answers will vary. Students might say that the artist believes that Bush is drawing attention to a problem that he created so that he can take credit for solving the problem.